REAL LIFE ZOMBIES

BY KRIS HIRSCHMANN

SCHOLASTIC INC.

D1408445

Photo credits:
cover, top right: © SciMAT/Science Source/Photo Researchers, Inc.; cover, bottom right: © James Thew/Shutterstock; cover, top left: © Cathy Keifer/Shutterstock; cover, bottom left: © Miguel Angel Salinas Salinas/Shutterstock; cover, bottom left: © Photolibrary/Getty Images; throughout, Halloween night backgrounds: © Migogo/Shutterstock; throughout, brain in a jar: © iStockphoto; throughout, gravestone: © Ruth Black/Shutterstock; throughout, world map: © Rafa Irusta/Shutterstock; throughout, exposed brain cartoon: © lineartestpilot/Shutterstock; throughout, rainy graveyard: © Tim Stapleton/Getty Images (RF); p. 1: © Science Picture Co./Getty Images; p. 2: © andrewshka/Shutterstock; p. 3, bottom right: © andrewshka/Shutterstock; p. 3, background: © Taddeus/Shutterstock; p. 7, right: © Kim Taylor/npl/Minden Pictures; p. 8, bottom left: © Kim Taylor/Nature Picture Library; p. 8, bottom right: © Nature Production/Nature Picture Library; p. 9, bottom right: © Gilbert S Grant/Getty Images; p. 9, top right: © Patrick Poendl/Shutterstock; p. 10: © argonaut/Shutterstock; p. 11, top right: © Cathy Keifer/Shutterstock; p. 11, bottom right: © sarah2/Shutterstock; p. 13, bottom left: © Simon Colmer/Nature Picture Library; p. 13, top right: © Simon Colmer/Nature Picture Library; p. 14, top right: © Florida Images/Alamy; p. 14, bottom left: © Marvin Dembinsky Photo Associates/Alamy; p. 15, top right: © studiomode/Alamy (RF);p. 15, bottom right: © zhugin /www.fotosearch.com; p. 16, bottom: © Jan Vermeer/Foto Natura/Getty Images; p. 16, top right: © dotweb/Shutterstock; p. 17, top right: © Nature Production/Nature Picture Library; p. 19, bottom right: © photowings/Shutterstock; p. 19, top right: © SciMAT/Science Source/Photo Researchers, Inc.; p. 20, bottom right: © David Scharf/Getty Images; p. 21, center left: © Steve Gschmeissner/Getty Images (RF); p. 21, top left: © Miguel Angel Salinas Salinas/Shutterstock; p. 21 bottom right © John Schwegel / Shutterstock; p. 21, bottom right: © Tristan3D/Shutterstock; p. 21, top left: © Photolibrary/Getty Images; p. 22: © Visuals Unlimited, Inc./Wim van Egmond/Getty Images; p. 23: © Science Picture Co./Getty Images; p. 25: © Jeff Rotman/Alamy; p. 26: © Dan Guravich/Getty Images; p. 27, bottom left: © Ted Kinsman/Photo Researchers, Inc.; p. 27, top right: © Ted Kinsman/Photo Researchers, Inc.; p. 28, bottom: © draganica/Shutterstock; p. 28, bottom right: © Daniel Heuclin/Nature Picture Library; p. 28, center left: © Seapics.com; p. 29: © Robert Valentic/Nature Picture Library; p. 30, top right: © andrewshka/Shutterstock; p. 30, bottom right: © Colin Cuthbert/Science Source; p. 31: © Klaus Guldbrandsen/Science Source.

No part of this publication may be reproduced, stored in a retrieval system, or transmitted in any form or by any means, electronic, mechanical, photocopying, recording, or otherwise, without written permission of the publisher. For information regarding permission, write to Scholastic Inc., Attention: Permissions Department, 557 Broadway, New York, NY 10012.

Written by Kris Hirschmann
Additional content by Greta Friar
Designed by YAY! Design

Copyright © 2013 by Scholastic Inc.
All rights reserved.
Published by Scholastic Inc. SCHOLASTIC and
associated logos are trademarks and/or registered trademarks of Scholastic Inc.

ISBN 978-0-545-53563-2

12 11 10 9 8 7 6 5 4 3 2   13 14 15 16/0

Printed in the U.S.A. 40
First printing, February 2013

Contents

They Won't Stay Dead!

The world is full of living **organisms**. They live for a while. Then they **die**. Then they **STAY DEAD**. That's the way it works, right?

Well, not always. Sometimes things come back to life. They groan . . . they stretch . . . they move . . . they **FEED**. You could say they're the living dead. Yep, that's right. They're **Zombies**!

"Zombies aren't real!" you may be thinking at this point. And that's technically true. The rotting, stumbling, brain-munching corpses of B-movie fame don't exist. **NEVER HAVE, NEVER WILL.**

But here's the twist! Some real creatures *can* survive **death**–or near **death**, anyway. They have the amazing ability to **slow** or even stop their bodies during tough times. They don't eat, or **grow**, or even breathe. They look completely lifeless. So when their bodies start up again, they appear to be coming back from the dead...just like zombies!

How and why does this work? It's pretty simple, really. Just like *moving* cars, living creatures need fuel. They turn things like air, *water*, food, and **heat** into energy to keep themselves alive. The more energy a creature uses, the more fuel it needs.

Let's go back to the moving car idea. How often would you have to fill 'er up on a long roadtrip? Lots, right? But what if you parked that same car in a garage and just turned it on now and then to keep the engine fresh? How often would it need fuel then? Hardly ever!

Creatures that can survive near **death** are like that. When they are near **dead**, their bodies use very little energy. This means they can do without air, **heat**, *water*, and other fuels they would usually need. As a result, they can starve, or **dry out**, or **freeze**, or survive other killing blows–**NO PROBLEM**! They just hang out, lifeless, until conditions around them improve. Then they crawl from their graves and go right back to whatever they were doing weeks . . . or years . . . or even **MILLIONS** of years earlier.

So what are these incredible organisms, and how do they do it? You're about to find out! In this book, you'll get close-up with our planet's living **undead**. You'll read about the amazing **adaptations** they use to turn death into life. It's extreme survival on display . . . and we're doing it in classic **ZOMBIE STYLE**!

Zombie TRICKS of the TRADE

Earth's zombies use scientific tricks to enter the dead zone. Here are the main ones.

Many animals, including bears, squirrels, chipmunks, and more, enter a deep, sleeplike state to get through cold weather. This state is called **hibernation**.

Other animals, including many insects and reptiles, enter a similar state due to hot or dry conditions instead of cold. This state is called **estivation**.

Some organisms don't sleep. They just slow way, way, WAY down. They barely eat, move, or breathe. They also stop growing and developing. This is called **dormancy**. It is generally an emergency response to stressful or life-threatening conditions.

Diapause is a growth break like dormancy, but it happens at specific times or under specific circumstances. It is a normal part of many creatures' life cycles. It's sort of like these organisms get stuck in baby mode for a while!

The most extreme zombie trick is called **cryptobiosis**. During cryptobiosis, an organism totally shuts down and shows no signs of life. It is as dead as it can be without actually dying. Some organisms can stay in this state for years before suddenly coming back to life!

You'll read about all of these strategies in this book . . . plus a few more. Get ready to get ZOMBIFIED!

CAUTION
Big Words Ahead!

Words in **bold type** are defined in the glossary on page 32.

BRAAAINNS!!!
These boxes contain fun facts, vocabulary words, and more. Just beware: bigger brains attract bigger zombies!

Look for the **BRAAAINNS!!** boxes at the bottom of each page to get extra smart.

Look for the **Resurrection Record** bars in this book. They show you how long the organism can stay "dead," using the tricks discussed above, before its zombie resurrection.

The longer an organism can stay "dead," the more gravestones it gets in the Resurrection Record meter!

Resurrection Record: The number in these boxes is the length of time an organism can stay dead at a SINGLE STRETCH. The organism might go through MANY such deaths in its lifetime.

CREEPY-CRAWLY ZOMBIES

Insects, spiders, and other wriggly critters live just about everywhere on Earth. Conditions on our planet vary wildly from one place to the next. This means that creepy-crawlers must deal with extreme cold, heat, dryness, wetness, and much more. The exact challenge depends on the critter's home environment.

Some bugs CURL up and die when the going gets tough. Others seem to die—but their "deaths" aren't real. They're just an extreme adaptation to changing conditions. The "dead" bugs don't have to cope with the heat, *wetness*, or dryness. When things improve, these critters rise from the dead . . . to live again!

This section spotlights our planet's creepiest-crawliest zombies. Get ready to die with a fly, swim with a shrimp, and log some Z's with a moth. You'll also freeze with a beetle and *drown* with a spider. You're guaranteed to be BUGGY about these amazing survivors!

WHO WILL BE RISING FROM THE GRAVE?

FLIES!
SHRIMP!
MOTHS!
BEETLES!
SPIDERS!

SLEEPING CHIRONOMID
(Polypedilum vanderplanki)

Location: Northern Nigeria and Uganda
Zombie trick: Cryptobiosis
Outlives: Extreme dryness, heat, cold, vacuum

THE BUG WITH 10 LIVES

Resurrection Record: According to one report, a chironomid stayed in a dried-up state for 17 years.

The **larva** of a type of fly called the sleeping chironomid is the **zombie** champion of the insect world. This little bug can **die** and come back to wiggly, wriggly life over . . . and over . . . and over again!

Where They Lurk:

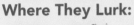

Chironomids live in central Africa, where the climate is mostly **hot** and **dry** with a brief *rainy* period. Chironomid larvae live in shallow pools of *water* that collect during this period. The pools **evaporate** regularly even during the *rainy* season. When the **dry** season arrives, they disappear entirely for eight to nine long, **blistering** months.

So why don't the larvae **dry** up and **die**? Actually, they do—but not for good! Sooner or later, *rainfall* creates new pools. *Water* covers the larval corpses, and a remarkable resurrection begins. The bodies swell as liquid floods their **shriveled** flesh. In only a few hours, the worms have recovered from their **deadly** adventure.

Time to breathe a sigh of relief? Nope! Those pools will **dry** and refill several times before the larvae reach maturity. Luckily, their incredible **death-defying** ability keeps chironomids alive during the killer **dry** periods they are doomed to endure.

Chironomid Larvae

BRAAAINNS!!!
Only chironomid larvae have zombie talents. Chironomid eggs and adults can't survive long dry spells.

ZOMBIE PETS!

BRINE SHRIMP
(Genus *Artemia*)

Location: Inland saltwater bodies worldwide
Zombie trick: Diapause
Outlives: Heat, cold, saltiness, lack of salt

Resurrection Record: Brine shrimp eggs have been known to hatch up to 10 years after they are laid.

Zombies posing as pets? You bet! These beasts lurk in toy stores all over the world. They're **dead** when you buy 'em ... but you can bring them right back to life at *home*!

The critters in question are called brine shrimp. They are sometimes sold under the brand name "sea monkeys." Wild brine shrimp thrive in *lakes* that are too salty for most animals. By living apart from **bigger** creatures, brine shrimp avoid being eaten by them.

This safety, however, comes at a price. Brine shrimp are so adapted to their homes that they cannot stand much change. They suffer if salt levels rise or fall. Low oxygen levels also hurt these creatures.

To protect future generations from these changes, brine shrimp lay tough eggs called cysts. The cysts are small, round, brown, and thick-shelled. They remain lifeless as long as conditions are bad—for years, if necessary. When things improve, CRAAACK! The cysts pop open, and a new generation of shrimp emerges.

It's a nifty trick. By waiting to hatch, these **zombies** guarantee themselves a healthy, happy "life after **death**" whether they're in the wild—or in your bedroom!

Where They Lurk:

under magnification

SALTWATER SURVIVOR

BRAAAINNS!!!

Brine shrimp cysts float! They sometimes collect in vast brown mats on lake surfaces.

brine shrimp eggs

YUCCA MOTH
(Prodoxus y-inversus)

Location: Southwestern United States
Zombie trick: Diapause
Outlives: Extreme dryness, heat, cold

SLEEP LIKE THE DEAD!

Resurrection Record: Yucca moths have survived 30 years in diapause.

yucca plant

Here's a **zombie** that takes its after-dinner nap seriously. One moth larva conks out after eating . . . and stays that way for up to 30 YEARS!

The big sleeper is a type of yucca moth. This insect's larvae hatch inside the fruit of a certain yucca plant. From late spring through midsummer, the larvae devour the fruit's flesh. Soon they are ready to change into adults.

Where They Lurk:

But **whoops**! There's a problem. Adult moths don't live long. They must mate and lay new eggs immediately. Right now, though, the summer growing season is over, and all the yucca fruit is old, **rotting**, and worm-infested. There's nowhere *good* to lay those darn eggs.

So what do the yucca larvae do? Instead of **growing** up, they zone out! They stay inactive until the following spring, when new fruit appears. Then the larvae revive, mature, and emerge as adult moths. They get right to work creating a new generation of **zombie** larvae.

That's if things go right, of course. **Desert** conditions are iffy. What if fruit *doesn't* **grow** for some reason? That's no problem! The larvae simply snooze until it does. Then they'll wake up to enjoy a fruity breakfast—and a mighty surge into adulthood.

SERIOUS SLEEPER!

BRAAAINNS!!!

Most types of yucca moths fertilize yucca plants. The ones that don't (like our zombie buddy here) are nicknamed "bogus yucca moths."

FROZEN SOLID!

UPIS BEETLE
(Upis ceramboides)

Location: Forests of Asia, Europe, and North America
Zombie trick: Freeze tolerance
Outlives: Freezing

Resurrection Record: Upis beetles can survive at least 6 months frozen solid.

Most animals struggle to keep themselves warm during the winter months, but not THIS zombie. The Upis beetle lets itself freeze solid, then SHUDDERS back to life with the spring thaw!

Upis beetles live in the world's northern woodlands, where winters are long and bitter. Temperatures plunge far below the freezing point and stay there for months on end. Conditions get cold enough to freeze blood and other bodily fluids.

This would be a death sentence for most animals. The Upis beetle, however, doesn't mind the cold one bit! This remarkable insect makes a natural **antifreeze** inside its body. When winter arrives, it fills its delicate organs with this substance. On the outside the insect soon freezes and "dies" . . . but its insides stay ice free and undamaged. It will be ready to *spring* back into action when conditions warm up in about six months.

How low can the Upis beetle go? Temperatures regularly creep below -50 degrees Fahrenheit (-45 degrees Celsius) in the Upis beetle's home **environment**. These bugs have survived even greater extremes in labs. You want to talk about cold, dead flesh? These zombies have it covered!

Where They Lurk:

ICE-FREE INSECTS

BRAAAINNS!!!
The Upis beetle's natural antifreeze is made mostly of a sugar called xylomannan.

WOLF SPIDER
(Arctosa fulvolineata)

Location: Salt marshes in Europe
Zombie trick: Deep coma
Outlives: Drowning

Resurrection Record: *A. fulvolineata* can revive after 40 hours underwater.

Seaside *marshes*, a type of low-lying grassy wetland, teem with life worldwide, but in parts of Europe they teem with the **UNDEAD**, too. The marsh-dwelling wolf spiders of this region can drown, then reawaken . . . just as good as new!

Where They Lurk:

Wolf spiders have developed this ability to help them survive in their *watery* homes. Salt marshes flood and empty with the changing tides. To live through flood times, when they get trapped underwater the spiders go into a state of deep **sleep** called a **coma**.

DROWN-PROOF!

Tidal floods usually last eight to twelve hours. In their sleep state, wolf spiders have no trouble lasting this long without air. They revive when *water* levels fall.

When removed from *water*, the spiders **dry** out and start to twitch. Soon the **zombie** insects are skittering around like nothing happened.

Scientists wondered exactly how long these insects could last without air. Lab tests show that wolf spiders can survive an *incredible* 40 hours underwater before drowning–drowning for real, that is.

BRAAAINNS!!!

Some spiders live underwater. They carry oxygen bubbles with them like tiny scuba tanks. They breathe air from these bubbles.

ZOMBIE PLANTS!

Plants and their relatives, fungi and lichen, have a problem: They can't really move around much. Okay, sure, seeds do blow from place to place. But for the most part, plants are stuck. They have to hang tight and take whatever nature throws at them.

It's a tough life being stuck in one place while getting pelted by the elements. But, hey, someone's gotta do it—and plants are well adapted to the job! These organisms have come up with ways to resist nature's nastiest tricks. They'll stop at nothing—even DEATH—when survival is at stake.

This section introduces you to some zombie plants and plant-alikes. You'll take a bath with plants and ferns, snooze with seeds, SHRIVEL UP with mushrooms, and even meet one organism that is actually two. It's gonna be one brush with death you'll never forget!

WHO WILL BE RISING FROM THE GRAVE?

SPIKE MOSS!
FERNS!
SEEDS!
MUSHROOMS!
LICHEN!

RESURRECTION PLANT
(Selaginella lepidophylla)

Location: Southwestern United States to Central America
Zombie trick: Dormancy
Outlives: Extreme dryness

DRYING WITHOUT DYING!

Resurrection Record: *S. lepidophylla* can survive at least 6 years of dried-out death.

The remarkable resurrection plant is named for its unique abilities. This **zombie dies** when conditions are dry . . . but moisture revives it to a healthy, blooming afterlife!

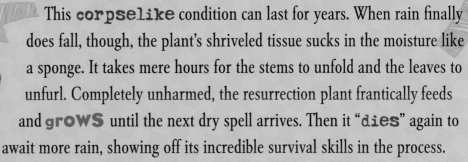
IT'S ALIVE!

Where They Lurk:

The resurrection plant is a type of spike moss. It lives in the **hot deserts** of the southwestern United States and Central America. Rain is scarce in these areas—yet the resurrection plant needs **water** to **grow**. How does it survive the long, bone-dry periods between rainfalls?

Easy. It doesn't! Or at least, that's how it looks. When moisture disappears, the resurrection plant starts to **shrink**. Its leaves turn brown and **curl** up. Then its stems **dry out**. Soon the entire plant **curls** inward to form a tight, dead-seeming ball of twigs.

This **corpselike** condition can last for years. When rain finally does fall, though, the plant's shriveled tissue sucks in the moisture like a sponge. It takes mere hours for the stems to unfold and the leaves to unfurl. Completely unharmed, the resurrection plant frantically feeds and **grows** until the next dry spell arrives. Then it "**dies**" again to await more rain, showing off its incredible survival skills in the process.

BRAAAINNS!!!
S. lepidophylla can lose 95 percent of its water content before dying for real. Humans get dangerously sick if they lose just 10 percent.

RESURRECTION FERN
(Polypodium polypodioides)

Location: Southeastern United States and southern Africa
Zombie trick: Dormancy
Outlives: Extreme dryness

Resurrection Record: Scientists believe *P. polypodioides* can survive 100 years without water.

The trees in some areas seem to wear bristling coats of dead leaves. These coats are armies of plant zombies in disguise. They're just waiting to rise from the dead and erupt into lush activity!

These freaky fronds are called resurrection ferns. Like resurrection plants, they shrivel to a crisp during times of drought and revive when it *rains*. They can endure this cycle over and over again without harm.

Where They Lurk:

The resurrection fern needs this unique ability to survive. Why? Well, this plucky plant roots on tree bark, so it can't take moisture from the soil. It has to get everything it needs from the air or from its host tree. *Water* doesn't last long on tree trunks, so the resurrection fern has to act *fast* when it *rains*. It gulps whatever moisture it can as rainwater trickles down the tree trunk. When the *rain* ends, so does the drink— and it may be a long time before another one arrives.

It's an iffy situation for sure. But it's no problem for the resurrection fern, which has adapted *beautifully* to its surroundings. By "dying" during dry times, this zombie survives to live . . . and live . . . and live again!

READY FOR RAINWATER

BRAAAINNS!!!

Once water is added, it takes a dry resurrection fern about 24 hours to come back to life.

PLANT SEEDS
(Many species)

Location: They're everywhere!
Zombie trick: Dormancy
Outlives: Practically anything, depending on the species

SPROUTING ZOMBIES!

Resurrection Record: One seed survived 2,000 years of dormancy.

Seeds may not seem particularly creepy, but don't be fooled. Many seeds exist in a **deathlike** state for weeks, months, or even years . . . before reviving and sprouting as **ZOMBIE** PLANTS!

Seed "**death**" occurs when conditions aren't good for **growth**. The seed senses this problem—and in response, it goes into limbo. A dormant seed won't develop or sprout even if it is planted. It just keeps on snoozing until something wakes it up.

Where They Lurk:

SLEEPING SEEDS!

So what's the alarm clock? It depends on the seed. Some seeds need **cold** or rain to revive, while others need **heat** or **dryness**. Some need light; some need dark. Some even need to be eaten by animals before they can come back to life.

Whatever the signal, it usually comes pretty soon. But things go wrong every now and then. For some reason the seed doesn't get what it needs, so it **sleeps** . . . and **sleeps** . . . and **sleeps**.

How long can it slumber? The record holder is an ancient date palm seed that sprouted after 2,000 years of dormancy. The tree is alive and well today in Israel. After milenniums of death, this incredible **zombie** is still **growing** strong!

date palm tree

BRAAAINNS!!!
A sacred lotus seed from China is another dormancy champ. This zombie sprouted after 1,300 years of death.

15

SPLIT GILL FUNGUS
(Schizophyllum commune)

Location: Forests worldwide
Zombie trick: Dormancy
Outlives: Dryness

Resurrection Record: The split gill fungus can survive 50 years in a dried-out state.

Taking a walk in the woods? Keep an eye out for the split gill fungus. Fungi look like plants, but they can't make their own food the way plants do. They can often be found on trees, feeding on their nutrients. When split gill fungi are *healthy* and well-fed, they focus their energies on making seeds.

Where They Lurk:

The process begins when underground fungi send shoots into the open air. These shoots are better known as mushrooms. Their job is to make seeds called **spores**. A healthy mushroom can pump trillions of spores into the air in a single **growing** season.

dried fungus

That's only if conditions are good, of course. Mushrooms need *water* to stay plump. If rain doesn't fall, they **dry** out. Most species **die** as a result.

But not the split gill! This sensational survivor just **SHRIVELS** during **dry** times. It folds inward to protect its seed-making parts. When conditions improve, the mushroom **swells** to its former size. It goes right back to shedding spores—and to creating a new generation of **zombies**.

BRAAAINNS!!!

Most living creatures have two sexes: male and female. But the split gill fungus has about 28,000 different sexes!

ELEGANT SUNBURST LICHEN
(Xanthoria elegans)

Location: Arctic and sub-Antarctic regions
Zombie trick: Dormancy
Outlives: Dryness, cold, radiation, outer space

Resurrection Record: Unknown. Scientists do know that the elegant sunburst lichen can live at least several centuries.

What if a zombie could make its own food, vitamins, and other essentials? The elegant sunburst lichen does just that. It uses this talent to survive practically anything!

Where They Lurk:

Here's how it works. The elegant sunburst lichen is actually a community of fungi and algae living together. The algae are plant-like organisms that make their own food and chemicals from sunlight. The fungi protect the algae. Everyone stays well-fed, healthy, and safe.

A ZOMBIE FAMILY!

At least, that's the case most of the time. The one thing the elegant sunburst lichen can't make is water. When things get too dry, the lichen faces the possibility of death. It shuts down most of its bodily functions and makes only what it needs to survive.

This ability comes in handy in the Antarctic. This region is a freezing desert with very little moisture. In places like this, conditions are rarely favorable. That's okay, because this lichen is a very patient zombie. It will spend a hundred years "dead" if it has to. When healthy, the lichen grows at the sluggish pace of a few millimeters a year. By living in slow motion, the elegant sunburst lichen survives the bleakest conditions on Earth.

BRAAAINNS!!!

The elegant sunburst lichen is tough enough to survive outer space. In 2008, scientists sent this lichen into orbit atop the International Space Station. The lichen was exposed to open space for 18 months and lived!

MICROSCOPIC ZOMBIES

Our planet swarms with organisms that are way too tiny for people to see. Germs, spores, and little crawling critters are everywhere. They're in the deepest oceans and on the highest mountains. They're in volcanoes and under glaciers. They're even inside your body. Gross—but true!

How do they do it? Well, these itsy-bitsy scraps of life have adapted over millions of years to handle all sorts of harsh stuff. The biggest test of all, of course, is death—but that's no problem for Earth's TINIEST survivors. These guys earn an A+ in survival . . . even if they have to DIE to do it!

This section puts some of these zombies under the microscope. You're about to bake with a fungus (really), get an intense tan, and time-travel into the past. You'll even come face-to-claws with an unkillable zombie—YIKES!! It's a CLOSE-UP look at a microscopic but marvelous struggle for survival.

WHO WILL BE RISING FROM THE GRAVE?

YEAST!
TARDIGRADES!
ROTIFERS!
BACTERIA!

BAKER'S YEAST
(*Saccharomyces cerevisiae*)

Location: Worldwide in warm to moderate climates
Zombie trick: Dormancy
Outlives: Dryness, heat, starvation

ZOMBIE CHEFS!

Resurrection Record: One ancient strain of *S. cerevisiae* revived after 45 million years!

Would you eat food baked by **zombies**? Sure you would! An **undead** organism called baker's yeast lurks in kitchens everywhere . . . including **YOURS**!

Where They Lurk:

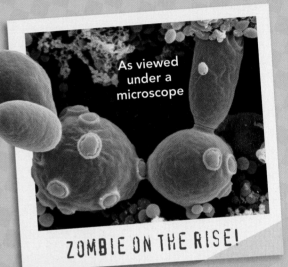
As viewed under a microscope

ZOMBIE ON THE RISE!

Baker's yeast is a very tiny fungus. It's too **small** to see without a microscope. It lives all over the world in **warm**, *moist* places, and it eats natural sugars. It makes a gas called carbon dioxide as it digests these sugars.

Yeast is very active under the right conditions. In **warm** bread dough, for example, yeast has all the heat, *water*, and food it needs. It eats like crazy and gives off tons of gas. The dough rises as gas bubbles form.

Conditions aren't always so perfect, of course. Yeast can't stand being too **cold** or too **dry**. It also needs a steady supply of air and food. If these things aren't just so, the yeast goes dormant to survive. It enters "off" mode to wait for a better time.

Thanks to modern technology, that time often comes in human kitchens. Bakers mix **dry**, dormant yeast with warm *water* and sugar (usually from flour) to crank it up. The yeast quickly revives and starts to feast. BRAAAINS? No. It's BREAAAD for this carb-loving **zombie**!

BRAAAINNS!!!
In the wild, baker's yeast often lives on grape skins, where it can feed on the grapes' high quantities of sugar.

TARDIGRADE
(Phylum Tardigrada)

Location: They're everywhere!
Zombie trick: Cryptobiosis
Outlives: Heat, cold, pressure, dryness, radiation, outer space

Resurrection Record: One tardigrade was revived briefly after 120 years of death. However, this record is debated among scientists because it died almost as soon as it was revived.

The incredible tardigrade may be the most successful **zombie** on Earth. This microscopic animal can endure almost anything in its "**dead**" state. Later, it will pop back to life . . . just as good as new!

Tardigrades are most closely related to spiders. They thrive in oceans, ponds, rivers, and other bodies of *water*. They can also live inside mosses, lichens, and other damp places on land. In short, wherever you find *water*, you'll probably find tardigrades. **Hot springs**, mountaintops, the ocean floor, the Antarctic plains, and much more–they all teem with tardigrades!

Where They Lurk:

Conditions can get pretty tough in many of these places. How does the tardigrade survive when things get too extreme? It doesn't! When life takes a turn for the worse, the tardigrade **CURLS** itself into a ball and stops its bodily functions. It rests in this **dead** state until conditions improve. Then the tardigrade twitches, **stretches**, and gets right back to business.

Many creatures use this type of survival strategy. What makes the tardigrade different is its unbelievable toughness. Scientists have tried to kill slumbering tardigrades with **heat, cold**, blistering sunlight, and much more. These **zombies** have survived it all. They're virtually unkillable–and THAT'S the scariest **zombie** trait of all!

Magnified 5600x!

HERE ARE SOME OF THE DEADLY TRIALS TARDIGRADES HAVE SURVIVED.

THE INCREDIBLE TARDIGRADE!

Temperature: Heat up to 304 degrees Fahrenheit (151 degrees Celsius)
Cold down to -328 degrees Fahrenheit (-200 degrees Celsius)

Oxygen: No oxygen for up to six months

Air pressure: Down to the near-zero pressure of outer space
Up to 6,000 times the pressure at Earth's surface

Dryness: Loss of 99 percent of its body water

Poisons: Full-body dunking in deadly chemicals

Radiation: 1,000 times the level that would kill a human

Outer space: 12 days of direct exposure to outer space

Magnified 250x!

THE ULTIMATE SURVIVOR!

MARTIAN ZOMBIES

Are tardigrades from Earth living on Mars? Maybe! Long-ago asteroid strikes on Earth threw up clouds of debris, including live tardigrades. Computer programs show that some of this material probably landed on Mars. Did the tardigrades survive the trip? If so, did they revive to become Martian zombies? No one knows for sure. But tardigrades *can* handle space travel, so it's possible. There's no telling what Earth exiles might be lurking in the Martian sands!

BRAAAINNS!!!
Tardigrades in their dead, curled-up state are called tuns.

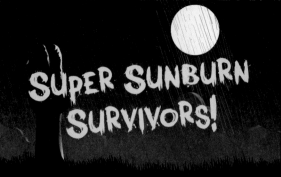

SUPER SUNBURN SURVIVORS!

BDELLOID ROTIFER
(Class Bdelloidea)

Location: Worldwide in fresh water and moist soil
Zombie trick: Cryptobiosis
Outlives: Dryness, radiation

Resurrection Record: Bdelloid rotifers can live in a dried-out state for at least nine years.

Bdelloid (pronounced DELL-oyd) rotifers are too small to see, but they have huge survival talents. These microscopic zombies can survive extreme exposure to sunlight, and they don't even use sunscreen!

Why did bdelloids develop this skill? Well, these creatures live in *water* and soil that shields them from the sun's burning rays. Sometimes, though, the bdelloids' homes evaporate. When this happens, the bdelloids let their bodies dry out. Near death, they wait for *water*.

Where They Lurk:

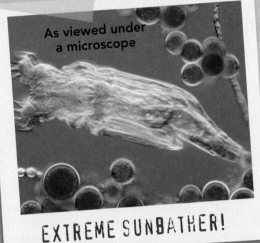

As viewed under a microscope

EXTREME SUNBATHER!

This waiting period, unfortunately, is dangerous. The bdelloid corpses can end up lying on bare, sun-blasted ground for years on end. How would YOU feel after that marathon sunbathing session? Yeah, you get the picture. You'd burn to a crisp.

But bdelloids don't. The same adaptations that let them dry out also protect them from sun damage—sort of. For most creatures, including humans, sun damage can lead to serious problems, like cancer. Bdelloids get fried by the sun just like everybody else, but they are able to repair the damaged bits of themselves as soon as they revive. This fixes the problems before they have a chance to become serious. It's an amazing ability—and one that lets this zombie survive conditions too hot for most creatures to handle.

BRAAAINNS!!!

Creatures that can survive extreme dryness usually have some sunlight tolerance, too. The abilities seem to go together.

ANCIENT BACTERIA
(Many types)

Location: New Mexico, Dominican Republic, Greenland, Alaska, Antarctica, and more!
Zombie trick: Dormancy
Outlives: Dryness, cold, heat

Resurrection Record: Bacteria have revived after 250 million years of death!

When it comes to sheer age, no creature on Earth can match the ᴛɪɴʏ but mighty **bacteria**. The best of these **zombies** can stay undead for hundreds of millions of years . . . then revive to **terrorize** a whole new era of history!

This *fantastic* feat begins when bacteria or their spores go dormant. They might do this because conditions are too dry, or too hot, or too cold for their liking. Whatever the reason, the bacteria "die" to wait for better times.

Where They Lurk:

So what happens if things don't improve? The bacteria just wait it out! As long as they're protected, bacteria can slumber for eons.

A strain of bacteria found in a New Mexico mine is an extreme example of this fact. The bacteria spent 250 million years trapped inside a salt crystal. Scientists rescued the dormant bacteria, which immediately revived in a nearby lab.

A few other bacteria are pretty darn ancient, too. A 40-million-year-old strain was found inside a chunk of dry tree sap. An 8-million-year-old germ popped out of an Antarctic glacier. And other old bacteria have come from frozen parts of Greenland and Alaska. Bacterial zombies are COOL customers for sure!

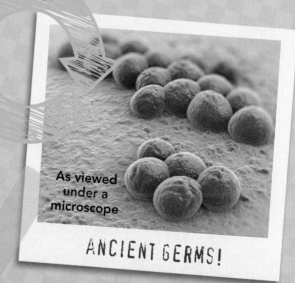

As viewed under a microscope

ANCIENT GERMS!

BRAAAINNS!!!

Some bacteria change their bodies before they go dormant to make them simpler. These super-tough, stripped-down bacteria are called endospores.

ZOMBIE ANIMALS!

Life in the wild isn't easy! There's only so much food, water, and shelter to go around. Animals must compete with one another to get these things. If they fail, they die.

Most mammals, fish, and other larger animals solve this problem the easy way. They settle in places with *comfy* conditions and plenty of resources. This cushy approach, though, is not for everyone. Some creatures SNEER at the lazy lifestyle and pick harsh environments instead. By doing this, they cut out the competition and keep more resources for themselves.

It's a smart but risky strategy. Earth's extreme animals may have less competition, but they face more survival challenges. In response, their bodies have developed some incredible adaptations. They can outlive anything—including DEATH!

This section gets *wet*, wild, furry, and slimy with our planet's zombie animals. Prepare to swim with a shark, sleep with a squirrel, and freeze with a frog. Get ready to take a zombie-infested walk on the WILD SIDE!

WHO WILL BE RISING FROM THE GRAVE?

SHARKS!
SQUIRRELS!
FROGS!
FISH!

EPAULETTE SHARK
(Hemiscyllium ocellatum)

Location: Oceans from Australia to Papua New Guinea
Zombie trick: System shutdown
Outlives: Suffocation

Resurrection Record: The epaulette shark has survived three hours without breathing.

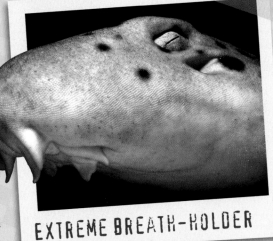

EXTREME BREATH-HOLDER

Without air, most creatures die within minutes. The epaulette shark, though, can survive hours of airlessness. This **zombie** seems to **suffocate** . . . but soon it wriggles back into action!

Where They Lurk:

This **astounding** animal roams the coral reefs between Australia and Papua New Guinea. It feeds in the tide pools that form when the tide goes out and *water* levels around the reefs go down. Like all sharks, it breathes oxygen that is dissolved in *water*. Coral produces lots of oxygen during the day, so everything is hunky-dory while the sun shines.

Nighttime, though, is another story. During low tide at night, epaulette sharks often get trapped in tide pools cut off from the rest of the ocean. Coral doesn't make oxygen in the dark, so until the sun comes up (or the tide comes in) the tide pool is limited to whatever oxygen is already in the *water*. The living things in the tide pool have to keep breathing, so they use up the oxygen. As a result, the tide pool's oxygen levels plunge. They can drop low enough to **kill** most fish.

But not the epaulette shark! This animal handles the air loss by shutting itself off bit by bit. First it slows its breathing and heart rate. It relaxes its blood vessels. Then it turns off the brain parts that control movement, vision, and other non-survival jobs. The shark seems to **die** and even starts to stiffen. But when oxygen levels rise, it revives with one desperate gasp.

BRAAAINNS!!!
The scientific term for natural waters not having enough oxygen to keep most animals alive is hypoxia.

COLDER THAN ICE!

ARCTIC GROUND SQUIRREL
(Spermophilus parryii)

Location: Canada, Alaska, and Siberia
Zombie trick: Supercooling
Outlives: Extreme cold

Resurrection Record: Arctic ground squirrels can spend two to three solid weeks below the freezing point.

Lots of animals sleep through the winter, but none quite like the Arctic ground squirrel. This **zombie** endures **freezing** temperatures . . . yet manages not to **freeze** itself!

As its name suggests, the Arctic ground squirrel lives in the Arctic. This region has long, **cold** winters. To survive these times, squirrels burrow deep into the ground. They enter a **deathlike** sleep called hibernation. Ground squirrels hibernate for seven to eight months each year. While a squirrel hibernates, it goes through an amazing change. Its body temperature **falls** . . . and **falls** . . . and **falls**. It may drop down to 26.6 degrees Fahrenheit (-3 degrees Celsius), which is below the **freezing** point.

Where They Lurk:

Yet the squirrels don't **freeze** into lumps of furry ice. How do they do it? Scientists aren't entirely sure. They have studied the squirrels, but they can't find any sign of antifreeze chemicals. Still, the results speak for themselves. The ground squirrel *doesn't* **freeze**. Okay, they can't stay **cold** the whole seven to eight months. They briefly wake up every two to three weeks during this time and **SHIVER** and **SHAKE** until they reach normal body temperatures of about 98 °F (36.7 °C). Then they go right back to **sleep**. They warm up for good when spring arrives . . . and the time comes for this **zombie** to rise from its chilly **grave**.

BRAAAINNS!!!

Ground squirrels save lots of energy by letting themselves get very cold. It's kind of like using less electricity to heat your house.

WOOD FROG
(Rana sylvatica)

Location: Northeastern United States, Canada, and Alaska
Zombie trick: Freeze tolerance
Outlives: Extreme cold

ZOMBIE FROGSICLE!

Resurrection Record: Wood frogs can freeze for more than four weeks without harm.

COLD AS ICE!

One "cool" **zombie** has real ice running through its veins. This monster has the awesome ability to **freeze** into a **dead**, **cold**, hard lump of flesh . . . and live to tell the tale!

Where They Lurk:

We're talking about the wood frog *R. sylvatica*. This animal is the only North American frog that lives above the Arctic Circle. In the winter, this region gets much too **cold** for most frogs to survive. They would **freeze** and croak—in the **drop-dead** sense, that is.

The wood frog, though, is different. When ice starts to form on this frog's skin, something amazing happens. The frog's liver pumps out a preservative liquid sugar. This sugar floods the frog's body. It protects the frog's cells and tissues from getting filled with **ice**, even though the rest of the frog is **frozen** solid.

What happens next? Well, the **frozen** frog just chills out until things **warm** up. Then it thaws and starts breathing. Soon the frog is eating and hopping around, as good as *new*. It's an astonishing recovery—but, then, this **zombie** is one of nature's most astonishing survivors.

BRAAAINNS!!!

The wood frog's heart thaws before its blood does!

AFRICAN LUNGFISH
(Protopterus annectens)

Location: Throughout Africa
Zombie trick: Estivation
Outlives: Dryness, drought

RIP RIP RIP

Resurrection Record: African lungfish can revive after four years of "death."

If you're walking in Africa, you'd better watch your step. The ground may look smooth and dry . . . but zombies hide below!

The dry-land lurkers are called African lungfish. These eel-like fish are born in swamps, creeks, and ponds. They thrive during the African *rainy* season, when there's plenty of *water* to go around.

Where They Lurk:

This cozy state, unfortunately, doesn't last forever. When the rainy season ends, things start to dry up.

The lungfish feels this change coming. In response, it takes *emergency* action. It burrows deep into the mud. It CURLS up and then spits out a cocoon made of mucus. Inside this slimy cocoon, the lungfish slows its body to near-death levels. It will stay "dead" until rain falls again, months or even years later. Then it will revive and wriggle out of the mud to begin its zombie afterlife.

SLIMY ZOMBIE COCOON

BRAAAINNS!!!
African lungfish need real air! They poke their heads out of the water to breathe.

STRIPED BURROWING FROG
(AKA GREENSTRIPE FROG)
(Cyclorana alboguttata)

Location: Northeastern Australia
Zombie trick: Estivation
Outlives: Dryness

UNDERGROUND SLUMBER!

Resurrection Record: Greenstripe burrowing frogs can survive at least five years without food or water.

The striped burrowing frog really digs the **zombie** lifestyle. It can spend long, **dead** years in a muddy hole before reviving . . . and rising!

Where They Lurk:

Burrowing frogs live in northeastern Australia. Dry, grassy plains blanket some parts of this area. Forests **grow** in others. Burrowing frogs swarm around the ponds that form there during *rainy* periods.

EFFICIENT ENERGY CONSERVER

Sooner or later, though, the *rain* clouds always drift away. Ponds everywhere **evaporate** as the sun beats down. When this happens, burrowing frogs dig deep into the mud. They shift their bodies into a unique energy-saving mode that does not waste a single scrap of energy.

Part of what makes the burrowing frog unique is that its muscles stay buff while it's in **zombie** mode. Many animals' muscles get **smaller** and **weaker** the longer they are not active. They have to use it or lose it! This is true of humans too, which is why athletes train constantly. But the burrowing frog's unique energy-saving mode prevents its muscles from getting **small** or **weak**, even when it doesn't use them for months at a time. This means the frog wakes up fit as a fiddle, instead of having to work itself back into shape after its **snooze**.

BRAAAINNS!!!

Instead of croaking, greenstripe frogs quack! They sound just like ducks when they "talk" to one another.

Zombies of the Future!

By now it should be obvious that real **zombies** not only exist, they're also tough almost beyond belief. These organisms just refuse to croak. Instead, they simply skip stuff that could **kill** them. Wouldn't it be great if people could learn how to do that, too?

Sure! But sadly, it isn't that simple. Human **corpses** may come back to life in **zombie** movies, but they can't do it in real life. Still, people **CAN** and **DO** dream of surviving **death**. Okay, we don't want to do it in an icky, drooling, movie-**zombie** way. But if humans could do it in the **NATURAL** way— the going-to-sleep, waking-up-normal way? Now **THAT** would be awesome!

Well, guess what? Scientists are trying to harness that awesomeness right this minute. They are busy studying our planet's real **zombies**. Little by little, they are finding ways to copy these creatures' amazing abilities . . . and, they hope, their sensational survival skills as well.

Want some examples? Of course you do. Here's a handful of **undead** trivia for you!

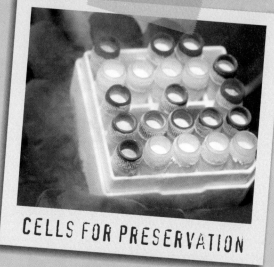

CELLS FOR PRESERVATION

CAUTION
Cool Science Ahead!

ZOMBIE SCIENCE IN ACTION

Medical Marvels!

- Organ transplants are tricky because tissue doesn't live long outside the human body. Zombie freezing techniques are now keeping organs healthy longer. This gives doctors more time to do their work.

- Another really COOL treatment uses cold and chemicals to revive dogs and pigs with extreme blood loss. This technique could save people with massive injuries.

- Scientists have made mice hibernate in labs. They can't do it with humans yet, but they're trying. Forced hibernation would be a big help for sick or hurt people.

Saving for the Future!

- Places called seed banks collect dormant seeds. Sometimes they also force regular seeds into dormancy. They store these seeds in case of future disaster. If an important crop or a rare plant were wiped out, seed bank "zombies" could start new populations.

- Places called frozen zoos do something similar for animal populations. These labs use careful chilling techniques to preserve tissue and egg samples. One day these samples could be thawed . . . and used to bring creatures back from extinction.

Sounds pretty cool, doesn't it? OF COURSE IT DOES. But that's the big picture. In the shorter term, people just want to SURVIVE—and that makes us just like all other living organisms. People want to keep living, even if they have to die to do it.

It sounds like a crazy movie idea, but it isn't. Real zombies do walk the earth. Organisms from bacteria to beetles and ferns to frogs have adapted to become extreme survivors. Nature shows us that it's just a matter of having the right tricks to outlive death. If scientists do research and experiment hard enough and long enough, who knows? Maybe someday WE can be death-defying zombies, too! Whether or not scientists figure out that trick, there will always be amazing real-life zombies out there. In the universal quest for survival, these organisms beat the odds by living on the edge of death.

Glossary

Adaptation: A special behavior or physical trait that an organism develops in response to its environment.

Antifreeze: A substance that prevents freezing.

Bacteria: Microorganisms that live in, on, and around most living and nonliving things. They are much too tiny to see without the most powerful microscopes.

Coma: A deep unconscious state.

Contagious: Able to spread from one organism to another.

Cryptobiosis: A state in which an organism shuts down normal functions and shows no signs of life.

Diapause: A normal part of some organisms' life cycles where growth and development stop, but very low body function continues.

Dormancy: The emergency shutdown of growth and development due to life-threatening conditions.

Environment: The air, water, minerals, creatures, and other things that surround and affect an organism.

Estivation: A deep, sleeplike state caused by dry conditions.

Evaporate: To change from a liquid state into a gas state.

Genetic: Having to do with genes. Genes determine an organism's physical traits and many of its behaviors.

Hibernation: A deep, sleeplike state caused by cold weather.

Larvae: Newly hatched, wormlike insects that have not yet changed into their adult form.

Microscopic: Too small to see without a microscope.

Organism: Any type of living creature.

Resurrection: The act of rising from the dead.

Spore: A seedlike object made by bacteria, fungi, and some plants. Like seeds, spores produce new organisms.

Suffocate: To die from lack of oxygen.